'John Davies is intensely conscious of life's value and he celebrates it in poems about his parents, in love poems and finally in elegies. In this gathering of work, we see a weighing up of what matters—family, freedom, friends, fun. Poem after poem explores what tenderness means. This is a life-enhancing collection that will surprise you and make you take stock. It is wise, unsentimental, honest and perceptive.'

Jackie Wills

'John Davies's fine volume of *New & Selected Poems* has the appropriate fizz, bustle and energy of small lives in nature. With equal facility the Shedman sheds and dons his alter ego as he traverses through childhood and adulthood, and through life's unpredictable up-and-down walkways. One of Davies's many strengths is the way he handles the ironic and the comic with exceptional ease and poise. This volume will make you laugh, reflect, mourn, forgive—but in the end it is a joyous affirmation of life's essential cycle that is worth the overall sojourn.'

Sudeep Sen, author of *EroText* (Vintage) and editor of
The HarperCollins Book of English Poetry (HarperCollins)

'There is a succinct swoop and dive to the orthography of this new collection by John Davies; one which can take in Walden's Pond with an aerial view before focusing on the subtle complexity of a seal carcass, a "flipper skeleton." The bird-like is everywhere; Davies alights and tugs at his subject matter, one eye on the reader, before flitting off again, and we are left curious, picking at the abandoned nest. This is a keen and affectionate ornithography of emotional values, cultural shifts. From bird-watcher to birdman, a poet's dawn chorus to the folk-song of the birds themselves, Davies pitches the familiar lightly and the everyday with evocative simplicity to sing "on a high branch in clear air."'

MacGillivray, author of *The Last Wolf of Scotland* (Pighog Press)
and *The Nine of Diamonds: Surroial Mordantless* (Bloodaxe Books)

'What Wordsworth did for daffodils, John Davies does for sheds.'

Nest

New & Selected Poems

John Davies

Red Hen Press | Pasadena, CA

Cover design by Jackson Rees
Cover image by Rosy McConnell
Typesetting by WatchWord Editorial Services

Library of Congress Cataloging-in-Publication Data

Names: Davies, John, 1950–author.
Title: Nest : new and selected poems / John Davies.
Description: Pasadena : Red Hen Press, 2018.
Identifiers: LCCN 2017018423 | ISBN 9781597097017 (pbk. : alk. paper)
Classification: LCC PR6104.A8645 .A6 2017 | DDC 821/.92—dc23
LC record available at https://lccn.loc.gov/2017018423

The National Endowment for the Arts, the Los Angeles County Arts Commission, the Ahmanson Foundation, the Dwight Stuart Youth Fund, the Max Factor Family Foundation, the Pasadena Tournament of Roses Foundation, the Pasadena Arts & Culture Commission and the City of Pasadena Cultural Affairs Division, the City of Los Angeles Department of Cultural Affairs, the Audrey & Sydney Irmas Charitable Foundation, the Kinder Morgan Foundation, the Allergan Foundation, the Riordan Foundation, and the Amazon Literary Partnership partially support Red Hen Press.

First Edition
Published by Red Hen Press
www.redhen.org

Supported using public funding by
ARTS COUNCIL ENGLAND

For Rosy

Also by John Davies

The Nutter in the Shrubbery (Pighog Press 2002, 2007)

Shedman (Pighog Press 2008)

Our Storeys: Art & Poetry in Healthcare
(with Sue Ridge, Pighog Press 2014)

Glove Poems (Editions Fuscus 2016)

The Stony Thursday Book 2016 (Editor, Limerick Arts 2017)

Contents

Foreword   xi

Nest   1
Blighted   2
Advent   3
The ward   4
Song thrush   5
Landscape with father   6
Signs   7
The permanent way   9
Dusk   10
After   11
Birmingham to Frankfurt inaugural flight   12
Ceramic   14
A game of catch   16
Baby, baby, where did our glove go?   18
The filling station   19
Invasive species   20
Gardener's question time   21
Welcome home Marena   22
Analogue   23
Independence song   24
Love poem   26
Channels   27
Glove handle   28
Words and lichen   29
Hawkish   31

Shannon   32
Campion   33
Cosy   34
Make believe   35
Shedman's missing glove—a sestina for Ruth   38
Kithe intaglio   40
What doesn't kill you makes you stronger   41
Walden life   42
… and counting   44
Bella de Noche   45
On finishing reading *Gilbert White* by Richard Mabey   49
Revenge   50
Spring   51
Winter   52
Ghosts   53
The ravishing   54
Happy   55
The beach seal talks to a tourist   56
Fish out of water   59
Open source   60
My island   61
The overgrown path   62
Clothes of grey   63
Oven gloves   64
Eden   65
Untitled   66
On the road   67
Paris census   69
Shedgang   70
Dragon   71
Halloween   72
Glove compartment   73

Getting Giuseppe to the airport   74
Loss of control   75
Maximum shed   76
The alchemist of the Athenaeum   79
Auscultation   81
Body mapping   82
9 lives   84
The doorway   86
Homecoming   87
Ariel   88
Earthed   89
Elegy   90
In memory of Beynon John 9.11.1923–6.4.2009   91
À la douce mémoire   92
Load   95
The big picture   96
The boy in the sunlight with the tousled hair   98

Foreword

John Davies comes across in his *New & Selected* Poems as a man of
ordinary things, and, as is appropriate for a poet with the alter-ego
Shedman, prominent among these is the shed. At the same time,
however, he likes probing beneath the ordinary, looking for the
essential, the *je ne sais quoi* which holds everything together, as in
his allegory of a doctor listening at the floorboards of a hospital
with his stethoscope, straining to hear the movements of the ghosts
responsible for 'the peculiar harmony of the whole machine'
('Auscultation') or again in 'Getting Giuseppe to the airport' where
he reflects on the infrastructure of ordinary life necessary for the
carrying out of our most taken-for-granted needs and projects.

He is, in other words, a poet of the meditated everyday and
emphatically not one of those whose 'unexamined life' is 'hardly
worth living.' On the other hand, he enjoys being surrounded by
gadgets and gizmos, brackets for curtain rails, the 'inlet probe and
the nozzle micromesh,' and doesn't at all mind cocking a snook at
portentous attitudes and cultural shibboleths. His ode to a glass of
coke and the 'borborygmi' it induces in his intestines is perhaps his
most obvious expression of sympathy with the non-sublime.

His poems deal with the joys and disappointments of ordinary
life, love, death, friendship, the bridging of generational and other
gaps through common interests, the bleak matrimonial wasteland
as well as the reverence that trust and continuance bring to love
partners, even the frustration of the needed but long-delayed cheque
and the pressure its non-arrival causes. Frustration of a more acute
kind stands up and declares itself in 'Glove compartment.' We are

given occasional quick peeks of transcendence in poems such as 'Gardener's question time,' which speaks of 'some interweaving he can't account for' in a familiar landscape.

To a considerable extent, Davies is a poet of landscape, of the British landscape (with a few glimpses of the River Shannon), its wildlife, and the history, both personal and pervasive, which landscape evokes. Some poems with urban settings are also tellingly descriptive.

Many poems evidence a quiet humour, while some provoke robust laughter. Davies's work often shows a yearning to break away from a sense of constriction, and this tendency is perhaps best illustrated by the poem 'Elegy,' which could be tagged as exhibiting the poet's 'Do not go gentle' strain: 'this elegiac tone really gets my goat.' ('Oh hell! Now the bloody bells have started!' as Jimmy Porter puts it.) On the other hand, '*À la douce memoire*' charts, detail by sadly tender detail, the dying of a female relative, while 'In memory of Beynon John' is a lyrically evocative 'list' poem, all the more affecting for its obliqueness. There is also the more inclusively pitched 'Love poem' which embraces Russia and elephants as well a lost *amour*.

What the above qualities amount to is the very welcome *New & Selected Poems* of a varied and layered poet.

Ciaran O'Driscoll
Author of *Life Monitor* (Three Spires Press)
and *A Year's Midnight* (Pighog Press)
Member of Aosdána

"The language of birds is very ancient, and, like other ancient modes of speech, very elliptical: little is said, but much is meant to be understood."

—Gilbert White, *Letter XLIII to Daines Barrington*
9 September 1778

Nest

It was when you went down the limestone steps
saying you might put a garden studio there,
but led me to the shrub in the centre of the lawn
where you pointed out a long-tailed tit's nest
constructed deep within the bush—
a little house inseparable from the body of the tree.
Like love, I thought, and its products.

Blighted

Hen-warm—held in her gloating—a child

she dismembers the memory—how he

the image always returns—his lip's quivering

of the broken—her look up—his words

how she feels at moments like these

betrayal, guilt, anger—something she should

have been responsible for—not broken

not out of control—the ovum—those words

procedure—dilatation—curettage

her husband's—silent—the ultrasound

empty—the yolk of a new generation

tainted—innards out—like screaming

next time he says—next time

Advent

Stalk, limb, sea scum, wrack—he scoops a clump,
binds it with plastic strands of pink and orange twine,
and over hours hides himself, reedy, worming,
within the capillaries of its mass, this redd, this birth rite.

In discomfort, that's where imagination poaches him,
etiolate, a filament of joy, a code of patient light,
anxious for the shadow's callous quickening,
though at its instant unawares. The eyed egg

on dream-watch sources smithing tongues,
hammer-works each scale of salmon song,
armour for the song of love and loss he
must sing from alevin to parr to smolt.

The ward

The cervix dilating two, five, ten ...
The blue avenue to the cream and Sharoe Green.
The quiet hospital and patches of dark,
footsteps of passers-by, children's artwork.

A curtain drawn back: welcome your
grandfather to your stage. Nursed
in your mother's bliss the star
that called us here, swaddled,

blinking, tiny. How simply exquisite
you are. How dare I—swamp
of experience—come to your cradle,
with adult faults so manifold?

Shall we protect you from the world
and all its miseries? Yet Brooke,
for all we know, a baby girl
may be the very shield we're waiting for.

Song thrush

This morning my mother's spirit comes to sing for me
from a tall elm, many years after her death. She sings
in the form of a song thrush on a high branch in clear air.

Or, is it the shade of a young woman I knew once on a ship,
who killed herself unwittingly. She sings from dawn till breakfast
and on towards eleven, though every note thrown to the suburb

so enthusiastically, reminds me of dream-waking to its sound
at daybreak, its clarion call, heaven on earth, so freely given
from its widened beak, and bursting speckled chest, calling.

Landscape with father

Laid out you became the hills
found here, the brown
flanks with stubble, slopes of scrub
and the wind-smoothed creases

in your forehead of grey stone.
An ochre thorp in your cheekbone,
an olive grove in the palm of your hand
grows over your fingers.

Now it's a warm season
above your feet. Playful
clouds welcome the coolness
of evening. Cooing
dovebirds sleepily nest
in the woodland of your hair.

As the rain comes this winter
it gets your eye lazily open:
here the clear water in the drought
that comes with summer. Children
spend hours pond-dipping
leaning over your lids.

What a surprise landscape. Had
you yourself ever thought you could be
that—so still at last?

Translated from *Landschap met vader* by Dutch poet Willem van Toorn

Signs

In the back of the Zodiac I watch you come out of your house
morning after morning, a given routine I have no real quibble with,
except its dullness, the Light Programme music of Bert Kaempfert,

the cigarette smoke, the greasy roads, the greyness of the Midland
city before the Rolling Stones or the Beatles, the queasy feeling in
my stomach from the Shreddies. It must be a particular morning

I remember because I always see the same sad sights, the floodplain
near the mine, the new aluminium extrusion plant, the old sandstone
river bridge, the railway bridge, the speedo ticking up to thirty, forty

but ready for the right-hand turn up your road, where you come out
of your house morning after morning, with a flower pattern dress,
a cardy, an unbuttoned coat, high heels, legs too good for your face,

glasses with little coloured wings on the top on either side, like waves
or the manes of toy ponies, buck teeth, badly cut hair; strange I
    remember
all this now. Why did I feel that particular morning was so important,

why does the image of the speedo stay with me, why can I see the curve
of the steering wheel and the profile of the businessman in the front seat?
Was this the morning it all started to go wrong as the dark blue Zodiac

cruised up the street and you stepped off the kerb for the nearside door
even before we had stopped. Was that part of the game to feel the door
swing open with the car still moving, you Catherine Deneuve

in *Les Parapluies de Cherbourg* or Audrey Hepburn in *Breakfast at Tiffany's*
and me just the kid in the back of the car? Who are you anyway?
We're on the dual carriageway and are you both talking or do you

stay quiet because of the boy in the back of the car whose view
is of the radio and the backs of your seats and the hands moving
together to the cigarette lighter? I'm really stuck. Was this the day

I got stuck? Stuck in the sixties coming out of the fifties, stuck with
a love of cold grey mornings and movement through suburbs
in a dark blue Zodiac, speedo ticking, at the wheel, a man I can trust.

The permanent way

The trains that ran here
no longer can, though rails gleam
in the moonlight, and some say
they hear the sounds of steam
locomotives heading up the glen,
the creak of signals changing.

We'd sit on the bridge,
wait for the up, arranging
when to take a breath, when
to let the damp cloud of motes
envelop our bodies, clenching
the cry in our throats.

Get the timing off you'd fight
for air. Get the timing on you
became one with the train, the
phantom of iron
that woke you at night,
turned young flesh to something
approaching machine.
We are what we dream.

Dusk

Before
    the blond child
        in the red crash helmet
had fallen
    in front of him
        from the scooter
            on the steep pavement
so close to the rush hour road

he'd seen it coming
scooped her up in his great spread of arms, had them outstretched
            a while before she fell.

Brave girl, he cooed.
She scowled
rubbing her elbow
in the half-light.

Her mum took a while
with her cigarette glow
and carrier bags.
He's a boy, she said.

I'm a boy, she said.

Well, he replied, there you go.

After

months of secret watching through his dad's binoculars
—just after school, one autumn afternoon, outside the green
mesh gates, whose sliding bolt defined the boundary between
the playground and the one-way street where parents stalled
    their cars—

he pounced, and took himself as hostage. 'Do exactly as
I say,' he said, and forced himself to cycle to the safe
house in the suburbs, checking all the way for any trace
of special agents, which he never saw, but wished he had.

'In all good conscience, why?' his prisoner tried to ask before
he phoned the local rag, and in a funny voice had claimed
responsibility. A puzzled telesales rep blamed
her boyfriend's brother. 'Little prick. Piss off.' The editor

just thought it all a hoax, even when the ransom note
arrived: *Dad, Pay Up or Else*. The hostage, subject to
all kinds of deprivation and abuse (he never knew
he had it in him), almost cracked, named names and times, and
    wrote

a signed confession. But he didn't. Instead he told him made
up stories, something like the ones he wanted him to tell,
and faced his bleak imprisonment like a man. Just as well.
There'd be no quick release. The ransom's still unpaid.

Birmingham to Frankfurt inaugural flight

His father is flying back from Germany that night
so when the thunder starts, the windows all flung wide
in summer heat, his mother, making raspberry jam
downstairs in the kitchen, transmits some taut anxiety,
an invisible signal, that flashes through the house,
one of the new semis built post-war, where cherry orchards
once stretched as far as the river bridge.

Seen from the sky, where even now a silver fuselage is tossed about,
the river's like a fat brown worm. Soon storm drains
and sewers will pump the worm fatter still with thunder water,
run-off from the city's streets, the new ring road's dual carriageway,
the airport's concrete apron and extended runway.
In the flood plain, while raspberry jam is cooling, boys lie awake
behind curtains closed to daylight at half past nine.
None can sleep, writhing on the static of the mother's nerve,
wishing father home safe inside the storm about to break.

And break it does, once the sky has turned to charcoal
and a giant cloud on a rush has made an anvil three miles high.
The plane battles on as if seeking the lost kingdom of Shangri-La
—or that's how the boys, who've seen the film, imagine it—
storm-tossed in the under sky, yawing wing to wing,
engines whining, trapped in the up-draught's gyre, inexorably rising,
though torrents surge downward from the great cloud's breach.

Through a drifting curtain the boy hears the first drops
land on leaves and tiles. Looking out, he sees fat slugs
of crystal juice explode in ones and twos on roof felt

and paving slab. Then on the leaves of ash and oak,
the rhododendrons, the red metal pedal car on the patio,
the glass roof, his windowsill, the rain drops drum and splash.
His face is electrified and moist and something
as old as Oedipus stirs, some longing mixed with dread.
Some hope salted with desire. What if, what if?

In a flash the storm's fulfilled, lightning rips the sky,
each thunderclap is overhead, the cloud burst vents its load
of drench into the valleys crease. On board the Frankfurt flight
businessmen are sick in small brown paper bags.
The German pilot wrenches back control from the rebel storm,
steers the plane into the rain shadow beyond the anvil cloud,
brings it in joking with his co- about a bombing run.
It comes to a stand in a dark puddle at the terminal,
where dismal lights make orange reflections rippled by rain.

At the storm's retreat the mother leaves the front door open.
His silhouette surprises her. Licking sticky fingers—
with the boys she's eaten doorsteps smothered in
summer butter and homemade jam—she kisses
his absence, asks how it went, if his secretary was all right,
how was the flight? In the hallway light, he's more positive,
holds up treasures from the trip, banners, beer mats,
a model tram, a perfume she has long admired.

Decades later, the dead father hails the son in a dream.
He seems happy, is typically pedantic about some matter,
but water pours over his ancient head, rivulets stream
down his thinning hair and lovely face. His son awakes
with a heavy pang. A slow tempest builds inside his mind.
He's knocked off balance, cannot forget that streaming head.
He weeps for love, and guilt, and remembrance.

Ceramic

There's a wall curving
straight through our hearts.
There's always a wall.

Each brick was carefully
placed in the wall that
curves through our hearts.

Knuckles were skinned
nails torn, hearts broken.
Men have died building

the wall that curves straight
through our hearts. And
the path along the wall.

We gather the children there
to celebrate our wall building,
to teach them our wall building

skills; to tell them the history
of the wall that curves straight
through our hearts, to keep it

in good repair. For without
the wall's curving, how would
they know which path to follow?

Stay close to the wall. Keep
away from the open land
beyond. The wall keeps us safe.

The wall curving straight
through our hearts
keeps us all safe.

A game of catch

Mum, the kids, Dad
caught and wrapped
in arms and kisses
NMUH
that's what this is.
All the patients'
comings and goings
all the visitors'
toings and froings
all the staff
on-call and off
all the movement
all the stuff
all the connections
all the skills
all the cures
for all the ills
all the kindness
and the care
all the knowing
someone's there
all the wipes
all the towels
all the instruments
and bowls
all the dressings
all the stitches
all the tears

all the kisses.
How we hurt
how we feel
how they answer
each appeal.
How the chase
is always on
how the chase
is never done.
How love chases
you and me
how we chase it
endlessly.

Baby, baby, where did our glove go?

Amidst the rusks and mortgages,
small arguments lay festering.
Hurts imagined as intentional,
unsquared by goodnight kisses.
Occasional nights of packaged sex,
otherwise grey dawns with dummies.

The children's primary school
the scene of petty jealousies and spite.
Whether his kiss was too affectionate
or she had too many male friends
on social media—it all took getting used to,
when no one was really used to it at all.

Year 5 was like a period of Pol Pot.
Their desire decapitated by arguments,
their relationship's decline reached Key Stage 2:
silence, shrugs and an atmosphere so bitter
the kids no longer cared.
One Parents' Evening it all came to a head.

The older lad was skipping class,
each blamed the other,
in front of all the school a stand-up row.
He slept on the sofa at his mate's.
Next day she rang the law firm up the road.
Gloves on or off, they never held hands again.

The filling station

She sees him from the booth
and watches with distaste
the way the nozzle kicks and spews
its froth onto the forecourt.

He's standing effing by the pump
feeling in his pocket for some change.
She flicks the switches
in response to angry buzzers.

She thinks of Sharon
who ought to be in bed
and Scott who's nearly three
crying in the cot that's wet again.

She puts two Mars Bars in her bag.
He's trying to screw the cap back on.
Now he's on his knees. It happened
Sunday night the same searching for the cap

as if he's lost the thing he values most.
The law would put him right, she'd see to that.
She wonders why he bothers, her ex-bloke,
hunting there beneath the signage.

Invasive species

Come the summer we'd gather sticks and chains
to thrash the knotweed, exported from Japan
to the field and copse behind our house,
all that remained of an ancient Doomsday woodland.
Its hollow stems reminded me of torture stories
from the Second World War, of how a man
would be immobilised above sharpened bamboo shoots.
The plants would burst in and through the body.
Using canes for bows my hand would often slip along a split.
How the bamboo cut, how the cuts would sting.
Inside each cane some white pulp
like the stuff inside the pods of ripe broad beans.
And, I imagined from my comics, inside the heads
of people too, bursting when the bombers came.

Gardener's question time

Astride the shed, he pulls the roof felt up,
gets blackened as he works. The radio's on.
A golden dog snoozes in the shade,
neighbours murmur just beyond the hedge.
Swallows dive and veer. A tower of cloud
billows from the distant horizon.
Something catches him that hangs him here,
for years—some nectar of the afternoon,
the heat, the sky, the birds, the Wiltshire light,
some interweaving he can't account for
yet feels so present in. It will encase
and hold him in a summer frieze,
that he'll go back to time and time again,
waiting for his daughter to appear.

Welcome home Marena

You stroll with her away
from the car in the sunshine.
Earlier, it rained. Grass is greener,
trees fresher. In conversation
you're already a man, relaxed,
limber. Your trousers flatten
to the movement of your legs,
the air fills the yoke and shoulders
of your shirt like pride.

A forest of white trees, the clouds
pile together swathing hillsides,
valleys, massive cliffs. The trees
surge in clouds, frothing
on the landscape, bobbling.
Behind you both, a flat sea
hangs like sky. In the clouds
enough blue to make
a pair of sailor's trousers.

Below, in the singular street
with its little painted houses all
of different hues, each connected
by wire to the telegraph pole,
a giant peg anchoring
a row of kites about to soar,
all anxiety's quelled in a footstep,
history shrugged so lightly
I hear the laughter of birds.

Analogue

Constance, newly arrived from her New York baptism,
tells me how she detests new maps. 'You know—
how you don't know where anything is. I hate that,
not knowing where you are.' After days of confusion,
she loves it when her map is worn with use, like her lover's
face, its topography revealing every step she's taken.

I watch the escalator climb toward departures
carrying an old man who may be going home.
I hate familiar plans with worn creases.
I long for a new map, to be seduced again
by its scent and texture, the teasing of new folds,
ecstatic to explore virgin territory with a finger.

Independence song

And aye and ayre, past Ailsa Craig we soared, the empty ship high on
    the wave.
In the deserted stern, my heart roared at its leaving, so isolate,
so proud, so explosive in the surface of the sea. Round the deck
    I ran to see it
from every angle that I could—the white vessel gliding by its mystery,
    soulless;
the sky indigo; the sea behind the wake of trammelled water,
    diesel-churned;
ahead the choppy, deep-sea glow of depth unfathomed. From there
    she rose
as certain as a goddess, solid in majesty, the awe of rock held fast. *Why*
this excitement? Then its loneliness, its solitary real-ness thrown at me
unexpectedly out from Greenock, on the dead man's run, me just a
    boy,
with all the hope of generations piled up against me as high as the
    Craig,
one thousand feet, as high as that, as if it had just sheared up from the
    water,
torrents fluming from its back, a sea giantess, Elizabeth of the Ocean.
And I thought I would top it, still do, but there she was as sudden
    as a goose,
out of the Clyde's reach on the Firth's edge before the Irish Sea, all a
    glory
of risen rock, fluted columns from one angle, a bun the next, and it
    was sunset.

There were birds feckless in the air. *What birds?* I couldn't name
   them but
they flew for me, all for me, and I was as isolate as the Craig, we
   knew that,
knew each other; call and response from each to each. Oh yes!
   Proud I was
of the Ailsa rock, for it was me, rising, and both of us gloried in our
   solo rapture,
you calling the rapture from me, a sudden partner on a lonely
   voyage. *How can*
you love granite? It has the grain of rebellion in its strata—sanctuary
   and exile.
I watched it sigh beneath the horizon. I watched it close, want it
   close even now
remembered, want that thrill and strange elation, discovery, suspense.
Yet deep within this monkish predilection, the ship, the boy, the
   English Cliff,
fearful and anxious right at the core, taut and unyielding, the sense
   of injustice,
the danger, the risk, the imagined stench of nature, the guano and
   mess: belief.
Who drove the ship? An unseen crew. Don't interrupt. We were
   together all at sea.
The rock and me, Ailsa Craig and I, the fairy isle and me. The rock
   of the sea,
and the isle of a boy, we were one in our isolate sovereignty. And
   that's the fear,
that escape not entanglement, that dream not real life; that boy, that
   rock, the puffins.

Love poem

How do you explain to someone you love,
that you love them,
when they never even give it a thought?

How do you show you love them,
when they're not looking?

How, for example, can I tell Russia
I love her, love the idea of her sense of self,
her huge expanses of territory,
her history and suffering,
when her behaviour is so dismissive, rejecting?

How can I show the elephants I love them,
fear for them,
love their intelligence and the idea of them,
huge, sentient creatures, mourning their loved ones,
helping each other?

How can I show love that acts, has agency, impact?
If only I could have told her
how important she was to me,
before that deluge submerged her in history
when I wasn't looking.

Channels

She sends me a message by Facebook
that pops up rather surprisingly, as I didn't know they could do that.
I reply to one of her ten different email addresses.
She sends me a tweet.
I send her a video, which was probably the wrong thing to do.
She answers with an email to all of my six email addresses
    including gmail and yahoo.
I give her a call on her mobile.
She doesn't answer but sends me a text.
I text back and for good measure ring her office number and leave
    a voice mail.
She responds by Pinteresting a photo of me.
I say what I think about this on Google Circles.
I receive a letter from her solicitor.
I ring her mobile and manage to get through, but she cuts me off.
Her solicitor sends me another letter.
I write on her Facebook wall what I think about solicitors.
She says I don't know how to communicate.
I say I never know where to find her communications.
She says I'm just avoiding mature communication.
I send her a picture of two fingers on Instagram.

Glove handle

The glug
is a cross
between
a glove
and a slug.
He stays
out late
at night
and drinks
too much.
He's a bit
of a mug
is the glug.

He says
hold on tight
to my glove
handle tonight.
I've a bucket
of love
to tip
over you.

Words and lichen

I can't explain how much I love you,
can't find the words for how I feel.
Words disappear beneath golden lichen
—what's said eroded by what's real.

Too late I know how much you loved me,
can't find the words for how I feel.
Love disappears when you scam for riches,
dishonesty destroys what's real.

Where the Shannon flows to Limerick
through valleys of green and gold,
I dream of you through summer sunsets
even though our love's been sold.

Sold my love to the highest bidder,
sold my love on a market stall.
Can't buy back the dreams of summer,
the money men have changed them all.

I broke your heart that cold December
moving money like children's toys.
I broke your trust, your self-possession
my greedy heart stole all your joys.

I watch the river unforgiven
by my wife and unborn child.
Cruelly lost in the dead of winter,
cruelly lost in the river wild.

I still go to that country churchyard,
still put flowers on your grave
and read those words in the stained glass
chiding me 'he cannot save . . .'

I can't explain how much I love you
can't find the words for how I feel.
Words disappear beneath golden lichen
—what's said eroded by what's real

Where the Shannon flows to Limerick
through valleys of green and gold,
I dream of you through summer sunsets
even though our love's been sold.

Hawkish

A military strategist, a scout,
his constant eyes would pierce armour, maps,
excuses. Softly spoken, yet the clout
to win the loyalty of all his chaps.

The jaw, above the turtleneck that traps
one collar wing, was resolute, the mouth
steel. But gentle the cradled hand that wraps
a pair of specs, worn since the move down south.

Now nested with his niece in Haywards Heath
(she's rescued many a wounded bird of prey)
he pinions the duality of truth,
with one wing trapped, the other flying free.

Swans pair for life. He'd swap every hour
of solitary flight to be with her.

Shannon

The wrap at her breastbone
could be the grey smoke
of the river's meander
through dusk in October.

The brooch at her throat
could be the gold serpent
that weaves towards sunset
seen from the plane.

That fall of black hair
could be the night river
seen by its sound
dark against dark.

I leave to return.

Campion

Glancing behind him through the open
French windows his focus would rest
on the crimson petals and grey green
fur of his favourite flower.

Undressed, she has just danced into
the garden, her natural home. Under
duress, he confesses the dreadful pain
of agrostemmas—the distress

of the plum juice campion
with duckling leg moss
of the whole garden growing
within him, a total mess.

Cosy

There's a nutter in the shrubbery
watching in the dark,
a face wreathed in laurel
eating laurel bark.

Arrived by air on Friday
nowhere else to go.
Asked to stay the weekend,
I thought that we said no.

Don't want the house observed,
nothing much to see.
We lead a pretty boring life
my catamite and me.

Make believe

I

In this fluid
they swap
objects
humans
they reach
inside me
I do not
I observe
reach to
the inside
of them
which is
always
turned
away from
me like
you.

Colour
shape
movement
depth
shade
oh now
I get it.

II

Wayside carmine juniper succulent
Rain and wind from the North
A dead field mouse on the path
Expect to be transfixed by turquoise
A clutch of jackdaws swooping
The western sun will light an eastern cliff
A cascade of primroses down a sea cliff
Seals will sunbathe below

III

The rocky promontory that holds the sky above the sea,
is just an image in my mind.

We disagree on colours, descriptions of the sea's angelic sparkle,
whether the rock be a whale fin,
how fast the gannet missiles to a fish.

Everything is up for grabs
a fluid field of processing
not one of us agrees upon
yet all agree there's something there.
All have that feeling.

There's me, making you and you me,
between us a glistening strap of hope,
once was expectation, now acceptance.

I don't want to deny it's not just an illusion
I want to believe I'm the being you make
becoming, not the being I've become.

Shedman's missing glove—a sestina for Ruth

I'm so confused I cannot hold new thinking
in my head for much more than a page, so all
my knowledge is partial, deliquescent in
a compost heap of ingrained mental habit
and ideas collected from God knows where.
Most seemed a good idea at the time so

I stuffed them in a mental drawer like gloves. So
now they're all mixed up, jumbling my thinking
with lots missing, important steps dropped somewhere.
When I try to communicate my thoughts, all
I transmit is the vagueness I inhabit,
a miasmic vapour deliquescent in

shimmering sweet nothings deliquescent in
goo. I envy those with firm opinions. So
logically solid is their mental habit,
their ideas feel like objects, their thinking
like express trains hurtling through the fog that's all
my own cogitation adds up to. Somewhere

I lost a winning hand. I wish I knew where
I lost it. My brain cells, deliquescent in
early onset Alzheimer's, or so it all
feels, aren't up for cerebration games so
the best I can manage with sloppy thinking
is write a poem, trying to inhabit

this little shed of form. Out of the habit
I may well be, but I'll have a crack, see where
things lead, whether poetry improves thinking,
or makes it even more deliquescent in
the Langolier erosion, creeping so
insidiously to make blanks of us all.

At best a temporary shelter from all
the shit, poetry's not the magic habit
found in Lady Wilde of Sligo's story (so
handy to disappear like that!) It's where
sound and rhythm turn us deliquescent in
all the strange stuff that's the ground of our thinking.

All I need is a poetry shed somewhere
to breed the habit of deliquescence in
writing and so find that lost glove of thinking.

Kithe intaglio

After Milton

Some thieving bastard's filched another year,
my fiftieth, and strands me still virgin
of fame, the hoped for Indian summer
kiddled with spoiled fruit: no foxes print
profit on my midnight. Lone on its beach,
long dead children argue and bite. Kittle
the elder's power that moulded each
lack, felt unvoiced by his eager, little
cadet, who loved and dreamed while anger made
its mark. The sooterkin, who're now my kith,
waif round me like felons; they tease and chide
me to day-labour. Dark, my fiftieth
is hell, a palimpsest my task mistress
abrades, hoping that what's to come is best.

What doesn't kill you makes you stronger

The single shoe that hit him had been fired,
with all the condemnation he inspired.
From toe to heel he felt its damning thrust,
the public's judgement on their misplaced trust.
The shoe's appeal—its golden buckle gleam,
its patent leather, a tantalising dream—
brought out the Cinderella in this con,
and, as any Cinders would, he tried it on.
The shoe fitted like a glove, and he could
finger count the reasons why it should:
calumny, hypocrisy, deceitfulness and grift,
not to mention his ugliness—something of a gift
to cartoonists and political foes.
But that, he told himself, is how it goes.
It seemed as nothing standing on one heel,
getting to know how a Führer might feel.
Although he hobbled, he threw back his hair,
watched each thrown shoe to make a matching pair.

Walden life

From Concord take the minor road that skirts the community gardens,
the court house and the primary school, and head out towards
    Route 43,
which travels East to Enfield, Windsor, Millfield Gap.

At the junction, cross the highway and enter the woodland through
the entrance marked 'No entrance.' Take the forest trail.
Beneath the moss, old stone scars. The trees whisper harmoniously.

Five minutes down the track, the noise of traffic at your back,
the rush of railroad steel ahead beyond the trees, you wind down
to a little pond and wonder is this Walden? Above the water's mirror

flies hover. The peaty bank shows evidence of creatures, a ripple
indicates a hidden fish. The stillness soaks up colour, texture, sound.
The mirror image drags time back. You could imagine you

as him, fretting at the disturbed stillness, searching for the place
to build the hut, wanting some sense of rightness in its placing.
He turns away and walks toward the patch of ground marked

by the blue sign: Site of House. You follow him, and understand
how well he chose the spot. Dappled sunlight falls through birch
    and larch.
A woodpecker rattles deeper in the wood. A jogger crunches past

and disappears, the sound as if recorded in a studio, the floor
a mesh of mast and needle, so soft it's like an animal's skin.
And you understand again what drew him in, what made him

stay. The hollow where the house once stood is nothing more
than a space inside the trees. Stone posts indicate the layout.
Where the wood shed stood, there's now a separate plaque.

Little stones brought in Thoreau's homage form a spreading
cairn, with names from Malmö, Bristol, Sarajevo, Kansas.
The ground slopes away towards a tiny beach and there,

in the leaves' vignette, a narrow vista opens on a stretch
of pale water. This is Walden Pond. Voices echo
from the swimmers on the farther shore, someone scissors

backstroke through the surface. A train heads towards
the depot and you imagine you can hear the clank
and hiss that he heard, above the engine of the stillness.

You circle round the site and think he wasn't far removed,
the town no more than twenty minutes' walk away,
his cabin like a shed on a garden's boundary,

a boy scout exercise rather than a hermit's solemn pledge.
And was it true that his mother used to come each week
to collect his washing? But here he wrote, writing out

his brother's dying in his arms from lockjaw, the tetanus
he'd contracted from a razor cut. In grief, the field and
forest gave him the sympathy of earth, as freely as

a mother's love. So he wrote out all his love and loss;
through the seasons, through the passing of the trains,
week in, week out, Thoreau's vigil at Walden Pond.

. . . and counting

There are twenty-eight shades of grey.
One for each day of the silver moon's turn.
Thirty, if you include the seagull sky seen
through the gap in the goose stone wall.
Thirty-two, if you add the pewter Ford Focus turning on the
    quayside.
Thirty-four! The dark shimmer of the cormorant's dive in the
    tide's race.
Thirty-five with the shadow of the knelt hill.
Thirty-six—the galvanised dull of the boat ring on the dock.
Thirty-eight, the mare on the famine road with its lichened wall.
Thirty-nine, the grike . . .

Bella de Noche

I

Beneath the spring board
beside the pool
water wagtails have built their nest.
One of the parent birds flies to and fro collecting food.
From the board three children
dive
and
jump
into the pool.

Tail wagging, a grub or morsel in its beak,
the parent bird approaches, then retreats,

The children tire and swim away.

The parent bird returns, mincing on its thin black legs.
Nijinsky-like it flutter-jumps inside the gap
between the stanchion   and the board.
The fat boy swims and splashes water at the bird.
I say, 'No.'

The bird comes and goes across the pool.
Its white breast reflects the turquoise water.

II

A young Italian, perhaps to impress his girlfriend
with his gentleness,

                lifts the board to view the nest.

       A parent jumps out tail flapping.
       From the dark beneath the board
       we hear whistling cheeps.

Now two birds fly back and forth
curling food in tiny beaks.

My wife and I question
the intentions of the man

                   on the floating lounger

who patrols the pool like a killer whale recceing for a hit.

The wagtail lands on an umbrella,
          clockwork walks the cream canvas
               then dives to sip the pool,
               its wedge tail gently fans the edge.

In silhouette, beneath the board are
        two fussing bodies,
        four unsteady legs.

III

Beside the old stonework of the wine-press room,
a plant grows whose name is Bella de Noche.

Its flower clusters of thin white trumpets open only at night.
With them comes a fragrance that longs to be described,
and held in words, but is as hard to catch as a bird.
To breathe the scent completely in the dark
is to be seduced by exotic dreams, 1001 Nights,
secreted in a film star's hidden room.
But before the nose or mouth or tongue or lip
can begin to guess the identity of any layer or note,
the perfume disappears.
My discrimination is as blunt as a pie.
A man's taste is what he trains it to be.

IV

Swimming in the pool I turn to see a great old dog
square-muzzled, heavy-footed, huge,
sniffing at the gap   beneath the board,
perhaps smelling a snack, or as pleased as we are
that a new family is getting started there.
He loses interest and shambles away like a slow black polar bear.

V

Now a parent bird is back,
                flying back and forth
                    above my head
                    jerkily pitching
up
    and
        down
through the bright air.

It lands on a parasol.
I watch her shadow strut across it delicately
until her head appears at the umbrella's edge,

                            where she watches me
head tilted to one side   then to the other.

VI

The day we leave, as I manhandle luggage down the stone steps
from our room, I see the wagtail sitting on a nearby roof.
It seems to twinkle at me, as though some flash
of something we can't possibly understand
or have forgotten
is watching me   and laughing.

On finishing reading *Gilbert White* by Richard Mabey

As clear as Christmas, I see the catkins she pointed out
on our nature walk along the lane behind the school,
finch-green with a secret yellow, dusted from the pores
and crevices of each tiny lantern-bell.

How high they seemed to hang to the children holding hands;
how gently bowed their branches to our ground.
Each catkin spoke of some direct connection
between the tree and the pet, the sound of trees, the purr.
So pussy-willow with its fur and little leather cap,
its white eye and straight limb, had to be some hybrid
in a world the catkins knew, but we could only dream of.
Although she knew. She took us there and showed us
something in the trees that had no name.

Like you, we wait for its returning every spring.
Some of us still think it worth a note in an email to a friend.
How the frogspawn sparkled in the pond in early March
but disappeared by Easter Day. How rarely now the swallows
fly above the house, and, whilst a blue tit fires itself
from the nesting box on the shed, how the heart aches
for a martlet in the eaves, or a nightjar on the evening breeze.

Revenge

In winter they burrow deep into the cloggy loam.
Concerned they'll suffer harm sometimes
she digs them out, and puts them in the shed.
The males rumble round like poltergeists,
disrupting stored equipment—tools, deck chairs
crashing to the floor. One year, fed up of their antics,
she re-entombed the lads. The females slept peacefully
in their beds of straw.

She scouts the garden, sensing something's wrong.
It's the season when the males yelp with lust.
Their tongues shoot from their withered heads like words,
harrying the females constantly, nipping at their heels,
pushing, biting, grappling, mounting them like stacking cups.

Hours later she's counted four. The fifth,
'1' in pink nail varnish on her back, is missing.
A low chicken wire fence surrounds a grubby pond.
She decides to dredge it, quickly trawls the missing shell.

Artificial respiration, coaxing the leathery neck with fingers,
airing cupboard warmth, do nothing to bring
her treasured tortoise back to life.
She curses the males, gathers them in a sack,
then takes a spade and buries them with her love.

Spring

Wait and see, the ancient tease: to soup
cooling on the canteen's steel top,
to boys who cannot sleep on Christmas Eve,
of prey the lion's yet to catch. Believe,
we're told, and all will be revealed, as if
we're children waiting for a treat like Spring.
But Winter light reveals an awkward truth
of half-truth, half worth waiting for, that's both
good and bad not either/or, etched
with uncertainy. The smiles fetched
through irony's despairing business day
by day mean more than any one can say,
save this: whatever you salvage of
yourself, treasure what you have of love.

Winter

Wait. Watch a scimitar of heath
chicane above the fencepost silhouettes,
careen along the hillside's windward crease,
as drab as the branches where it settles.
Wait. See the ground start up and fly
and leave its long-legged shadows in the snow.
Observe a wing of primrose in the sky,
how long it takes for anything to grow.
Wait. Count dull barbs on silver wire,
sodium stars that pierce the closing dusk,
wheat stalks scorched in the harvest fire,
the total sum of humanity's flux.
Will waiting help us understand how much
of us is there, how much of there is us?

Ghosts

Where the path ended
in the crush of stalk and brier,
dozens of cartridge cases:
blue, green, orange,
red and brown,

reminders of the gunmen
who wait here year on year,
as the crop is harvested,
eyes keened to the unsheathed edge.

The hands of men steady
as the harvester goes round and round,
the sun setting and rising,
the guns spilling colour to the ground.

The ravishing

As connected to the season
as the mesh of nest and birdsong
and the warm afternoon closeness
of elderberry, nettle and cow parsley,
a boy plays at the base of a broken tree,
tumbled in a storm many years before.

In a reverie he digs at the giant hand
of roots. Golden soil cascades
in showers. Suddenly, he's pinioned
breathless on the stump by a force
freed from earth or thin air,
with its sear, soul-tear, ambition.

Then it's gone, adrift across
the rosebay willow herb,
towards the railway, the drainage pipes,
the tennis courts and playing fields,
towards the entrance to the lane
enrapt in bread and cheese.

Happy

Walking with the golden dog
along the path from Sennen,
the stack of granite high above
the primrose and stitchwort,
swallows writing letters in the sky,
zipping in and out of dimensions,
a cuckoo on the cliff laughing,
the path winding the dog along the cliff
to the other beach, where heavy
in the sand the seal's torso lies
headless, holes neatly pecked
into its sides, flipper skeletons,
its dead weight on the tide mark,
its wreck of fur, shit and blood,
and the dog there rolling, rolling
with a kind of glee.

The beach seal talks to a tourist

You thought I was dead didn't you? As you came down that
slipway I heard you say 'Oooh' and you saw me as a dead
seal. Why did you do that? Do you want me dead? Have you
murderous intentions on seals? Or do you assume any
animal lying still with its eyes closed is dead? Is that
sentimentality, or ignorance, or both?

As you can see I am not dead. But then you thought perhaps
I was injured or sickening. You imagined the great shielded
turbines of submarines chewing my flesh, or a bash on the
head from a passing cruise liner—as if only men ever do
anything to nature and human agency is the most active
ingredient in the universe.

I'll have you know I'm not dead, not injured, not sickening.
I'm OK. Better than OK in fact, I'm lying here pleasantly
dozing, taking things mi-ghty slow, having a bit of fish now
and then as I wish, but I don't eat too much, just what I need.
The rest of the time I lie down. Like now. I enjoy my sleep
and you're disturbing my peace.

Isn't there a law against that sort of thing? Not helped by
the aggressive colours of the anorak you're wearing.
You want to be noticed as you walk on the cliffs. Me—I
don't care if I'm noticed or not. In fact as I lie on the beach
I can honestly say I don't want to be noticed. That's why I'm
this whitish grey-green colour

like a guano covered rock or a fall-out shelter. I'm always
grateful not to be woken when slumbering. You thought I was
dead, didn't you? Which shows how rock-like I can be. And
you'd like to get closer now, wouldn't you, with your 18 mega
pixel Canon 7-D and it 50–500 millimetre zoom lens.
Well, why not use that zoom?

You won't need to come any closer and my sleepy cosiness
will be preserved. I'm so comfortable. I couldn't give a sardine's
fart about the flies on my belly or if you are David Attenborough.
I'm a one-eye closed kind of seal, rather than the one-eye open
sort who are always pleased to see people and play with balls.
I like diving to the deep of sleep or sea.

Any time spent in the sea's gloaming will tell you how short
life is—especially for fish—how long the eyes stay shut or simply
don't exist. I think it's our natural state really, non-existence. So
it's worth enjoying the being here, even though you took me for
dead—or injured—or sick—and thought perhaps I needed water,
considered dragging me back to the sea

down the sandy trail made by my flippers and tail where I hauled
myself ashore for the pleasure of the doze. But you hesitated,
imagining the teeth of a grumpy seal, the bite marks in your arm.
A good decision on your part, not to pull me down the sand
by my tail, roll me like a carpet or a barrel towards the wavelets.
My one eye is watching you

but would rather close. I wave a flipper in your direction. You say
how sweet, he's saying hello. Quite the opposite. So allow me to
ease back to my pleasure, its fugal delight. There, have you got
your shot? Surely by now. How many digital images of a sleeping

seal does your computer need? It'll look fantastic on Facebook.
Now I'm being snapped on iPhone

and will soon appear on Androids and Blackberries the world over.
My snooze on the beach has gone viral in seconds—a YouTube
star for a minute or two. I would rather nod off. Rest my heavy
muzzle on the lovely damp sand, sense the firmness of the beach's
slope against my girth, feel the stretch of my carcass to my tail.
You thought I was dead, didn't you?

But I am not. I am alive, but asleep. I am diving deep. I am.
Or I was,
until you came by.

Fish out of water

The mermaid may appear
whatever time the tide,
whatever hour the lock gates
shut the harbour pool.

Her face may rise through oily swell,
when all of us are loading
or unloading cargo, hiding
contraband with a shifty look.

She'll play a while, then I'll meet her
at the harbour steps, lift her bodily,
dripping wet, smelling of whelk
and estuary, let her soak my jeans

and shirt and face,
her hands around my neck.
The weight of her against me,
I kiss her salty breasts.

She leans her forehead
close to mine and, murmuring,
encourages my hand
behind her tail. I turn her

on my lap and with both hands
slide her gently, wishing
I could follow, back where she belongs,
back where she belongs . . .

Open source

For Petina Gappah

The river where she swam was not her own,
its source lay far from where her limbs had grown,
but where it bathed her in its open code
the river's reach was broad and multi-flowed.

Even in the mountains of its source
snow-melt mixed deep permafrost in its course.
Each tributary added sediment, torque.
Man-made culverts braiding nature's work.

She knew fluid dynamics, understood
water's quaint qualities and quantities;
she loved its babbling stream, its pooling spell.
Immersed in it, as right as rain, she would
hug herself, accept the river's fealty
to its new engineer. It kenned her well.

My island

The silence is broken by the silence itself
something else is listening
except at night, when crabs
in their millions scriggle on the shore.

I take the green pill first and spend a day
lost inside an engine made of glue.
In the water there's a woman's face,
a giantess who stretches deep across the bay.

When the rain is warm I wash;
when cold, I hide,
imagining the buckets
I do not have, filling to the brim.

The knife I'd hidden when I took
the drugs, I cannot trace.
The beach smells of sisal,
damp earth, salt, and something else.

Lying down, my eyes next to the sand,
I watch the insects' traffic.
By day I try to catch the crabs
I hear at night, but never do.

The boat fizzes to the dock. I step aboard.
On the other side of the trees,
nothing is happening.
Nothing I can see, anyway.

The overgrown path

I meet these characters in
clearings edged with mist,
on paths through bracken,
their heads swathed in rags
like soldiers from the front.
Scarce words are said.
Beyond the swish of wind
I often hear a cry and stop
to ponder.

When safe inside our cabin
in the woods—blessed by pets
and your presence—the figure
in the bed, surrounded by our
children, sheets still warm,
pale butter on the table,
the smell of coffee and
baking on the air,
you wonder

why I seem so ill at ease
and though I laugh, so
rarely celebrate. I guess
a part of me can't believe
it's true or isn't here, or
can't forget the sizzle of
raindrops on leaves, the
tramp of feet through trees.

Clothes of grey

The dusk gathers the riders. Do not compare yourself with these.
Why, they feel nothing. Do not dwell or hanker. Do not follow
    their
clothes of grey, your vanishing mist, slipping through the trees.

Why do they call you when my love gives you opal, cockatiels,
    keys
to open and enlighten secret rooms. Why sing in the shadow
    where
the dusk gathers the riders? Do not compare yourself with these

poor things, they are not real. Where will they lead you? Please
look at me. Where am I in your plans? Tell me. How am I to share
clothes of grey? Your vanishing mist slipping through the trees—

is that all I will have and hold of us? How can you? How she's
lost him, they'll say, as if I've been careless, when it's just not fair.
The dusk gathers the riders—do not compare yourself with these.

When will you come back? When will your heart unfreeze?
If not for my sake then think of the children. Must they wear
clothes of grey, your vanishing mist? Slipping through the trees

without a word, you coward—you think escaping frees?
We'll see. I'll wear grey silks, the finest underwear. I don't care
the dusk gathers the riders. Do not compare yourself with these
clothes of grey. Your vanishing? Mist slipping through the trees.

Oven gloves

Long gloves, said the Ancrene Wisse, were not for holy women.
In Bologna in 1294 samite gloves were banned,
as perfumed gloves were in Rome in 1560.
The Ditchley portrait of Elizabeth
shows her left hand holding leather gloves.
What symbolism there?
By 1592 the Queen of England had made gloves
the accessory to die for.

Talking of death, how often in films do we see the killer
—strangler, assassin, gunmen or guard—
wear black leather gloves.

They did in Auschwitz—*all the regalia necessary*
to convey a power impossible to challenge.
Those gloves asked a question: *is there an appropriate time*
in which to lose one's family, one's community, or one's life?

The italicised quotes are from *Auschwitz—The Evil of Man* by Peter Kleinmann

Eden

I loathe/adore this boxed-in landscape
field/clouds brown/chalk

a searchlight scabious
amongst the fumey wild thyme

chacking birds in sour trees
trunks/fenceposts lichen yellow

the smudged textile of sky/land
sunlight the colour of needle

stitched with coltsfoot gold
edged with blackthorn sculpts

over some brow the wind flaps
full tilt from the north/east

veils of cloud/smoke
skin-pinning rain

body/raiment clothe
it's tempting to hope

Untitled

Shack amidst willows: swan amongst ravens
stooping on the rim of an icy marsh area.
Beside it through the vista: the great road to Ljubljana
plunges away from Ljubljana, zooms into evening.

No uplighters shine gaily from the bays.
Quite soon this construction melts into obscurity.
Say, the proprietor and his woman spent their days . . .
Say, busy life may . . . Say, good sense might . . .

The dark gorges itself on the image;
just leaves a miserable snowless season.
Or, say if the lord of misrule,
or the salt-tasting wind came ambling by . . .

And say, but one spark burst into flower,
say one crystal were to be snared by the lights
of a car, say it was swerving . . .
Say, just reachable . . . Say, white might . . .

Translated from *Hiška med vrbjem* by Slovene poet Milan Jesih

On the road

That grey enormous night en route
to Scarborough in Trevor's mini van
to see the eastern sunrise on the Winter Solstice.
Seven of us scraped together the petrol money
for the trip from Morecambe,
but the cigarettes ran out halfway there
and no one could have prophesied the cow.

We came across it in the fog,
and the motorcyclist dazed beside it,
helmet askew, goggles cracked.
I 'it the bluddy thing, he says.
We ought t' move it.

We liked the 'we.'

He's tentatively pulling at a hoof.
Black and white, the cow is huge and dead.
The fog is closing in.
I imagine every HGV in the North of England
bearing down on this section of the A684.

Seven students and a motorcyclist,
who says *It's got the bloat*
as if he's knowledgeable about such things,
try and move the beast.

But the four on one side
must be pulling harder than the others.
The carcass tilts like a capsizing yacht,
the legs wheel over and the cow's stomachs
hit the tarmac with a flabby slap.

A zeppelin of gas escapes the corpse.
A smell the size of Yorkshire encompasses the group
who stagger about arms outstretched, like victims
in some weird zombie horror.

Worth a try, the motorcyclist says after something of a pause.
Then, as headlights crest the brow,
he mutters darkly, *But mebbe not.*

Paris census

- There's a man with a gammy leg
- There's a man wearing an orange shirt
- There's a woman wearing a brown hijab
- There's a guy wearing a turquoise shirt
- There's a little girl with a white scooter
- There's a woman wearing faded denim jeans
- There's an old man walking along the gutter in grey trousers
- There's a broken bike leaning against the bike stand on the corner
- There's a man in a Paisley bandanna standing by the greengrocer's
- There's a dog with a large white protective collar around its neck

Shedgang

We are what you hide.
You can't come in.
Don't even think about it.
You'll find nothing.

We know who you are,
even when you don't.
We talk about you
and all your stuff.

We know what we want.
What you forget, we don't.
We congregate on backroads,
hatching plots.

Dragon

It's sitting in the corner of your shed,
sad eyed and legless. 'You love me,' it says.
Many's the day you've ignored its mournful look,
crossing the threshold from what once was
to what might have been. 'I love you,' it says,
and tries to get up on its little stumps, but falls.
Sometimes you pick it up; more often watch
it crawl back to its patient corner where it moons
for days. 'Love you more,' it simpers. In its eyes
flash a hundred dreams, their promise just about
to be fulfilled. The day you turf it out, it glowers
at you, silently, in the hatchback to the dump.

With acknowledgements to Brian Patten's *A Small Dragon*

Halloween

The promised cheque doesn't arrive,
the fax and printer misbehave.
Spam trickles down the screen,
waiting for the phone to ring.

There's work to do but none that pays.
'Try B & Q,' your partner says,
'where you got that bloody shed—
three months since you last got paid.'

Hemmed in by that pressing wall,
the shed looks the way you feel.
Inside you think you've seen a ghost—
could be the future not the past.

Glove compartment

In his cubicle he feels like Dilbert in his frame,
stuck between Analysis (Finance) to his right
and Help Desk (Europe) on his left. Driving
home, wedged between an Audi and a Volvo
in his 03 Nissan, he mistimes a turn, ends
up stranded in a cross-hatched square.
My life's like this, he thinks, watching other
drivers lose their rag. Every night sandwiched
between his Mrs and their eight-year-old,
who's having trouble sleeping on his own.
Weekends hemmed in by visits to ageing
parents and giving lifts to step-kids he has
never really known. His dreams are filled
with empty spaces. But when he wakes,
before he hides behind the cereal at breakfast,
the thought occurs to him in the smallest room,
how pretty much all life ends up in some kind of box.

Getting Giuseppe to the airport

Number 1 in a series

Have you ever realised the effort involved
in getting Giuseppe to the airport on time?

That an airport was there to be on time to, for a start,
let alone the infrastructure of the power generation system

and the rail network that delivered him to the sky gate;
and just as important, the industrial base that had to exist

before alkaline batteries could turn the hands of the alarm clock
made in Japan that woke him in Italy; and more significantly,

the fact that Giuseppe woke up and got out of bed at all,
reasonably conscious of what he was doing,

although not feeling on top of the world.

Loss of control

The line supervisor tonight is Derek.
He controls the five tanks of colour,
the pumps and nozzle apparatus
and the bodies on the robotic jig.

In Shafi's absence, it's Dean who sees
the jaundice sickening the silver.
Somewhere between the inlet probe
and the nozzle's micromesh, there's a prob.

They pause the process, check the gauges.
Derek doesn't understand. Dean suggests
a foreign body, or a hose that's hampered.
Start it up again and see what happens.

The change occurs within ten seconds.
A purple the colour of maggoty berries
squirts from the sprayers onto every profile.
Not in this year's range, says Dean.

Derek jabs the stubby shutdown button
but nothing happens. Worse—
everything that could go wrong
does.

Maximum shed

For Max to mark the opening of his new shed

Let's go down to the shed again, my old mate,
Let's go down to the shed again and talk until it's late,
till the bottles lie empty in the grass
and stars fill the sky.
We'll put the world to rights, you and I.

Do you remember those rainy days,
school in Builth Wells?
The old library, the cigarettes
and those inaccessible girls?

Forest brought us together,
Forest took you to Notts.
Forest draws us together again
in spite of all they've lost—

that unbeaten League game record,
the glory days of Clough.
Supporting the Reds over the years
has been surprisingly tough.

But through them we've won our friendship,
stronger as each year goes by—
though now your shed's bigger than mine,
I'm starting to wonder why?

And Max, what a shed you have for yourself
a maximum shed at a stroke,
somewhere to carve your name with pride
—and enjoy a sneaky smoke.

Though you may have sown the seeds of change
allowing a drum kit inside.
Still, amidst the snare and the high hat
young Pepe can follow your lead

and learn the arts of the shedman,
those moments of solace and grace.
(We'll forget the odd occasion
when you've been off your face.)

Those times when the wind seems to listen
as the afternoon curls into dusk,
when words between friends aren't needed
and nothing is too much to ask.

Gone are the days in West Bridgford
with the old allotment shed,
where you spent so much time inside it
you never grew any veg.

No apples, no courgettes, no marigolds,
just weed as thick as thatch.
That's when the old folks decided
to drum you off their patch

But now—you've got a shed to be proud of,
with room for your cat, dear old Laugharne.
Now I guess you won't be away so much
in your Volkswagen camper van.

But how do you solve a problem like Maria?
She's the love of your life no doubt.
But a word of advice from me and the shed
put a sign up: *Women! Keep Out!*

Let me say, once for all, it's a pleasure,
and an honour I'll never forget,
to be asked to cut the ribbon
to open the way to your shed

Here's me in banking and finance,
you a psychiatric nurse.
No doubt we'll be friends forever,
even beyond the hearse.

And whatever we've shed to get here,
whatever we've shared in the past,
let's shed much more in the future
and share a full life to the last.

So, let's go down to the shed again, my old mate
Let's go down to the shed again and talk until it's late,
till the bottles lie empty in the grass
and stars fill the sky,
and we've put the world to rights, you and I.

The alchemist of the Athenaeum

There we met in the clubhouse
next to Psyche's naked stone.
Peter had the Lemon Sole,
John the Dover off the bone,
Paul—the venison, Martin—grouse,
all enjoyed the wine, a Rhone.
All are well, though looking older,
all are now well past three score.
Girths are greater, waistbands tighter,
hair is greyer, wrinkles more.
They all go home full and happy,
tucked in bed they start to snore.

Martin's liberal generosity
sustains each glad reunion meal.
Never a question of repayment,
save the gratitude we feel
for the kindness of a school friend,
the character his gifts reveal.
Astute and loving every challenge,
smart and sharp, afraid of none,
honest about his motivation—
taking care of number one.

Yet through his store of wealth and fortune
a rare magnificence has shone.
A caring heart that's kept well hidden
as if shielded from the world by lead,

better to disguise empathy
with the mask of a harder head.
But each of us knows that lead better,
not base metal, pure gold instead.

Auscultation

Lying on the floor with his stethoscope
he's listening to the sounds of the giant,
the wheezes and rhythmic thrummings,
the crepitations from deep within its bowels.

The organs of the leviathan murmur
in all their separate compartments.
Beneath the Marley, lurking in the subways,
dodging staff and patients, there are ghosts.

They congregate for a fag outside the lift
machinery room, play hide and seek inside
the sub-station, take turns to slide the ducts.
Their real business is something other.

They orchestrate the engine of the hospital,
the xylophone of its spinal corridors,
the bruit of its wings and arteries,
the pulse of arrivals and departures.

He's lying on the floor with his stethoscope,
listening to something beyond the individual,
the peculiar harmony of the whole machine,
though colleagues question his unorthodox approach.

Body mapping

Waiting for his taxi in reception,
weighing up the signs,
he thinks about the hospital as a body
made of all the different bodies
he's seen treated here, including his.

Upstairs are the *Private Parts*,
where he had his waterworks
examined by cystoscopy.
Just thinking of it
makes him desperate for a wee.

Next door on the ground floor is the *Leg*
—though he can't remember if it's right or left—
the fracture clinic where Ken had his broken tibia
(or was it fibula?) put right.

Down the passage on the other side
is the *Head*, where dozens queue everyday
to see the ophthalmologists as best they can.
He's stared back at many an unknown watcher
on the wrong end of a telescope,
with someone squeezing chilli in his eye.

The *Arms* are the maternity unit
where Julie gave birth
to his grandaughter in a bath.
He wasn't allowed in, until, on the final push,

Ken had somehow slipped and broke his leg.
So Granddad was the first to hold *Charlize Pascal*
now known as *Tommi*, while they got her dad
disentangled from her mum and the umbilical cord.

He navigates the hospital by body parts
and sits now in the *Mouth*
with a cup of tea from the WRVS.
He imagines leaving with a giant's gentle kiss.

9 lives

Now when I hear that music,
I want to sing along,
be part of what they're singing of,
be something in the song.
To be the boy who fought at Bute,
or died at Donegal,
to take aim on the Turkish beach
and be the last to fall.

It's one for the history.
One for what you're told.
One for the wishful thoughts.
One for getting old.
One for the dream of heaven.
One for the heart that's young.
One for God and one for the cause.
And one for the song that's sung.

Which life would you like to lead,
the soldier or the squire?
Which part would you like to sing,
the solo or the choir?
To be the lonesome trumpeter
across the fields at dawn?
Or the massed bands of the legions
before their ranks are torn?

It's one for the cabin boy.
One for the lad called Tom.
One for the terrorist.
One for the homemade bomb.
One for the dreams of freedom.
One for the ancient call.
One for the living, one for the dead.
One more and I've used them call.

It's one for the heresy.
One for how you're conned.
One for distraction.
One for the distant blond.
It's one for the bet, one for the drink.
One for the whole night long.
One to keep for the one you love.
And one for the song that's sung.

One to keep for the one you love.
And one for the song that's sung.

The doorway

The photo shows him half-hidden
by the door he's painting as if about
to pass through or push to closed.
His smile has that smile older men
wear like well-worn trousers soon
to be discarded. His limbs seem
angular, thinner than the year before.
He's remembering the summer day
his own father stepped across
a daisy lawn holding out a black
masonic case, saying, 'It's all here,
everything you need to know, if
anything should happen.' Today
he realises time has him in its sights
and very soon, after a ruthless clearing
out, his own children will hold
some small container of his stuff.

Homecoming

For Meela and Trish

You're home from hospital next week.
I'm fixing brackets for curtain rods
in the downstairs room that will be yours.
I use my father's tools, the few I took
after his death just weeks ago, and on them
are his hands, his eyes, his breath.

These curtains will hang, be opened, close,
day after day. Sometime towards the end
of summer your mother will step
into the kitchen to make a cup of tea
pulling the curtains to behind her,
thinking of picking up the phone.

From your house, in the far distance
I see the Chattri, white on the Downs.
Where the streets end, reflections from cars
twinkle in the haze like tiny stars.
The suburbs glaze in a blue silence.
You're not yet home, though soon will be.

Ariel

For Michael Donaghy

The night-flyer caught coming in low
and fast with words as munitions
each laser-guided to its target,
the meaning in us.

Professionals look up to him.
Star performers feel out-performed
by his trick of memory and gentleness.
In the spot his body seems to hover.

A cold stage. A dowdy mackintosh.
Brilliant colours helix in the expectant air.
The voice quiet with love, the words homing,
the song enduring, the audience airlifted.

Earthed

The day I sheltered there, there was no snow,
though snowy hair and winter thoughts had drawn
me up past Tilton Wood and Pearson's Wish.
That autumn day I lay down at the foot
of Bostal Hill, a miniature of all that lay above,
and cried away my grief and all my love.

The rhythm of the chalk, its roll and turn,
holds me in a strong and timeless trance,
the comfort of the ground beneath Bo Peep
and Jerry's Pond. She who once was frozen
stone naps now in the hill, the giantess
asleep before she wakes to dance.

Elegy

For Kevin Elyot

I know it's sad, all this going,
I have the English dread of change,
want it always all the same—
prefer to channel loss, not growing.

This elegiac tone really gets my goat,
everything shrouded in sentimental mist;
poems written in the aftermath, the poet pissed.
I think it's time to grab elegy by the throat

and shake it hard, that from its strangled cry
we might detect what poetry it really has to offer.
Or whether these mourning togs and poseur coiffure
simply camouflage the fear to die.

So when you left with ne'er a word and friends
who loved to see you had no chance
to bid adieu, have one last hug or dance,
what use is elegy? I think what you preferred

was viper wit, gossip and news of all you knew,
tidings of great adventures destined to fail,
anything that let you weave a tale
to regale your friends, who can't believe it's true.

There is no more of you.

In memory of Beynon John
9.11.1923–6.4.2009

Feathered cirrus strafed by contrails,
American light, layered between bush
and tree by birdsong, the rippling bird,
the seagull, the chinking tit or chiffchaff.
The young Korean with her boyfriend,
she smiles; the single-engined plane
heading west, the cumulus roiling on
the far horizon beyond the Downs,
the plume of the great enemy
on the march towards London.
The blond dog watches a magpie.
A woman helps a Staffie climb into
her camper van. Two women, one in
a baseball cap, pause to talk nearby.
The dapple of the dark wood. Sleep.

À la douce mémoire

In memory of Tricia Veeren

There's always a train jolting into a distance,
the sound of summer rain on summer roofs,
a woman in an upstairs bedroom curled
upon a bed hunting breath.

They came and went, came and went,
throughout the week like the trains
she heard at night. Her sister bore the burden
of the woman curled upon the bed.

The district nurse came four times a day.
The home hospice team set up camp.
The woman curled upon the bed
the focus of employees across the town.

She knew her future, the woman in the bed,
a matter of days, took the trouble to order
chocolates for a favoured in-law,
brought her nephew to tears with kind words.

Day by day they came and went, the carers
and the hospice team. All the while the sister
stayed stroking hair, holding hands,
talking of younger days and stuff that binds.

The curl of the woman in the bed began to slide
away from consciousness, the sister saying

it was safe to go, to join the daughter dead
seven years and all the loved ones.

And slowly faded the woman curled.
She clutched me close one afternoon
wanting nothing more than a stroking hand
and music to see her through.

So before the woman curled in the bed
let the drugs do their work,
her hands flew across the screens
of phones and iPads seeking Finzi

or McKeller or Aled Jones or Water Music,
until the sister took the technology
from her hands and settled on Faure's
Requiem, and the little body lost in the bed,

hunting breath, hardly the breath to scrape
a cough, punished with back ache,
IBS, bed sores, all but a skeleton,
restless, hands plucking at her shoulder,

curled into a small package for oblivion,
believing in angels and an afterlife of sorts.
(Her nephew said it could be wonderful
to return as a tree or a swarm.)

The little body barely spoke at all
when an old friend called by.
The hospice team returned again
gave her morphine, eased her pain.

They gently rearranged the bed.
The woman could lie quiet now
held in her sister's valiant love.
She never awoke, was restless for

a while longer then, when no one
was looking, stopped hunting breath,
changed colour and was gone.

Load

An imaginary lorry,
a juggernaut stacked with stuff,
takes the turn badly,
runs out of road.

The wheels lift,
the whole caboodle tilts,
sheds its load.

The year on its turn
scatters its stuff,
its left-behinds,
across hedgerows, fields.

The year goes on
laughing.

The big picture

I'm staring at my Coke
as bubbles appear from
nowhere. Is there a frogman
in my drink? A frog?
Unlikely in cola.

The bubbles follow
each other in a squadron
then weave to dodge an ob-
stacle. An exclamation mark
balloons above my head.

Oh! I say. Deep within me
empty spaces form
that you can't see.
Hunger pains?
Indigestion?

Anxiety more like—
about what's in my drink!
My colon groans again.
Curdling, wordling, burbling,
borborygmi rise.

I can't stop imagining
what's going on inside,
these hidden things I feel.
Rumblebelly. Collywobbler.
Christ, I'm scared.

If what's inside
keeps seeping out
slowly through our lives,
seen in the cinema of the universe,
do we just go pop?

The boy in the sunlight with the tousled hair

comes up to me at the gate and says,
'Nice bike.' We compare notes.
His has thirty-six gears.
Mine just eighteen.

'In one you can go up any hill easy,' he says, before pushing off.
Stuck on the back he has a stick with a flag,
a skull and crossbones,
black and white on a bright red background.

A blackbird sings.

It's one of those days when adventures begin.

Acknowledgements

The following poems are reprinted with kind permission from the publishers:

After, The filling station, Analogue, Campion, Cosy, Kithe intaglio, The ravishing, The overgrown path, Getting Guiseppe to the airport and *Loss of control* were first published in the pamphlet *The Nutter in the Shrubbery* (Pighog Press, 2002, 2007).

Advent, Signs, Welcome home Marena, Hawkish, Walden life, Fish out of water, My island, Clothes of grey, Shedgang, Dragon, Halloween, Maximum shed, Auscultation, Body mapping (as *Mapping the Body*), *9 lives, Ariel* and *Earthed* were first published in *Shedman* (Pighog Press, 2008).

Ceramic, A game of catch, Spring and *Winter* were first published in *Our Storeys: Art and Poetry in Healthcare* (Pighog Press, 2014).

Baby, baby, where did our glove go?, Glove handle, Shedman's missing glove—a sestina for Ruth, What doesn't kill you makes you stronger, Oven gloves and *Glove compartment* were first published in *Glove Poems* (Editions Fuscus, 2016).

The ward was written to celebrate the birth of my first grandchild, Brooke Ingleson, 18 October 2014.

Landscape with father and *Untitled* were translated during the 8th International Golden Boat Poetry Translation Workshop at Škocjan, Slovenia, 2010.

Ceramic, A game of catch, Spring and *Winter* were commissioned by Bouygues UK through First Aid Art as part of the *Our Storeys* Poetry Wall Project at North Middlesex University Hospital, Lead

Artist Sue Ridge.

Gardener's question time was first published on www.yorkmix.com

Hawkish was written as part of a project working with Arundel Writers Group and Arun Artists.

Campion was first published in the anthology *Ice on the Wing*.

Shedman's missing glove—a sestina for Ruth was written in response to a challenge from my daughter, Ruth Davies. 'Langolier' refers to Stephen King's novella *The Langoliers* in his 1990 short story collection *Four Past Midnight* and made into a TV mini-series in 1995.

Fish out of water was first performed with a musical accompaniment by Phil Roberts and was published in *Dreaming Beasts* (Krebs & Snopes, Chichester).

A version of *Open source* was first published in *The Irish Examiner*.

Clothes of grey was read at the graveside of Slovenian poet Srečko Kosovel (1904–26) on Sunday October 1, 2006 as part of a short series of reading by attendees at the Apokalypse Review in Review meeting, Dane 2006. Meela Veeren, my niece, died on September 23, 2006, age 22.

Shedgang was written as part of Shedman's first project, the Achi-TEXTS residency at the Booth Museum of Natural History in Brighton curated by Mark Hewitt.

Dragon and *Halloween* were first published in *The Shed* magazine.

Maximum shed was written as a special commission from Jonathan Bridgeman for his oldest friend Max to mark the opening of his new shed.

The alchemist of the Athenaeum was written for Martin Leadbetter.

Auscultation and *Body mapping* were written as part of *From the Outside*

In, a Shedman residency at East Sussex Healthcare Trust with visual artist Sue Ridge supported by Arts in Healthcare.

Homecoming was first published in *Poetry South-East* (Frogmore, 2010).

Earthed was written as a response to the photograph by Margaret Weller LBIPP as part of the Footwork event at The Crypt gallery, Seaford, in December 2004.

In memory of Beynon John 9.11.1923–6.4.2009: The title is taken from a memorial plaque on a park bench in Withdean Park, Brighton, home of the National Lilac Collection.

À la douce mémoire: My sister in law, Tricia Veeren, died on August 22, 2013.

I'm very grateful to:

Judith Watts at Kingston University Press in the UK and Kate Gale and Mark E. Cull at Red Hen Press in the US for publishing this collection.

Dr David Rogers for choosing the poems and for his editorial guidance, Linda McQueen for her design and typesetting of the collection and Victoria Blunden for her careful project management.

Brendan Cleary, Ciaran O'Driscoll and Jackie Wills for reading and commenting on these poems at various stages of their development.

Arts Council England for a grant to support the launch of this collection.

With very special thanks to my wife Rosy McConnell for her unfailing love and support through all poems, all times.

John Davies

Born and raised in Birmingham in the English Midlands, John now lives in Brighton on the south coast.

His work has been published in *The Guardian*, *The Irish Examiner*, *The Echo Room*, *Poetry South East*, and *azul*, amongst others, as well as online. He was the first non-Irish editor of *The Stony Thursday Book*, an annual anthology of contemporary poetry published in Limerick.

John is perhaps best known as his poetic alter ego, Shedman (www.shedman.net), the original itinerant poet in a shed who has appeared at numerous festivals and events. As Shedman his commissioned work has ranged from poems engraved into the windows of a learning centre on the Cambridge Biomedical Campus, to major hospital projects with artist Sue Ridge, to a poem about the Forest Ridge for the High Weald Area of Outstanding Natural Beauty, emulating Michael Drayton's alexandrines in his Poly-Olbion.

www.johndavies.net

Printed in the USA
CPSIA information can be obtained
at www.ICGtesting.com
JSHW080001150824
68134JS00021B/2215